MY BOOK OF HAPPINESS

MY

BOOK OF HAPPINESS

THE BEATITUDES FOR CHILDREN

Eileen Lomasney, CSJ   art by Alice Hausner

Publishing House
St. Louis   London

To my sister and brothers

Library of Congress Cataloging in Publication Data

Lomasney, Eileen.
    My book of happiness.

    SUMMARY: Explains in verse the joys that can be ours by
living well, as set forth in the beatitudes.
        1. Beatitudes—Juvenile   poetry.   (1. Beatitudes—Poetry.
2. Conduct of life—Poetry) I. Obata Design (Firm) II. Title.
PZ8.3.L847My   811'.5'4   76-3616
ISBN 0-570-03455-8

    Concordia Publishing House, St. Louis, Missouri
    Copyright © 1976 by Concordia Publishing House

    Manufactured in the United States of America

When Jesus lived in Galilee,
A long, long time ago,
The people loved and followed Him
Wherever He would go.

They followed Him from dawn till dark,
Up high, green hills and down.
They'd find Him by the lake He loved
Or in the crowded town.

They brought Him all their sick and blind,
And those too lame to crawl.
Some who came were sick at heart—
And Jesus healed them all.

But He did much, much more for them
And more for us, His friends—
He brought GOOD NEWS of *happiness*
And *love* that *never* ends!

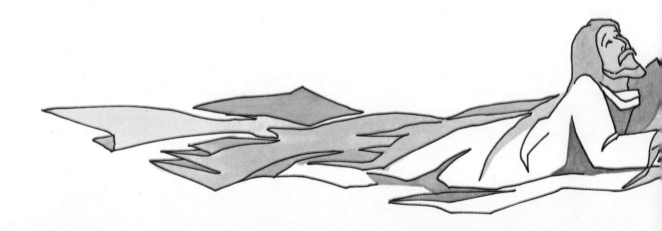

HAPPY ARE THOSE WHO KNOW
THEY ARE SPIRITUALLY POOR;
THE KINGDOM OF HEAVEN
BELONGS TO THEM!

How happy are those children who
Give joyful thanks and praise
For every good and precious gift
God gives in human ways:

The gift of life itself: the love
Surrounding us each day
In Mother's arms, in Father's hug,
In friendship when we play:

For eyes to see a mountain,
A bluebell, or a star:
For ears to hear a kitten purr
Or birds sing free and far:

For hands to help and comfort,
Or share (pay loving heed!),
The food and clothes we've plenty of
When some poor child has need.

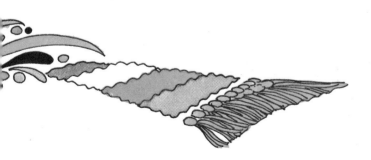

And for our brother, Jesus,
The best Gift of them all;
Without His love to guide us
We're poor, and weak, and small.

How happy are those children who
Give thanks for all these things,
For heaven is most surely theirs—
And theirs, a heart that sings!

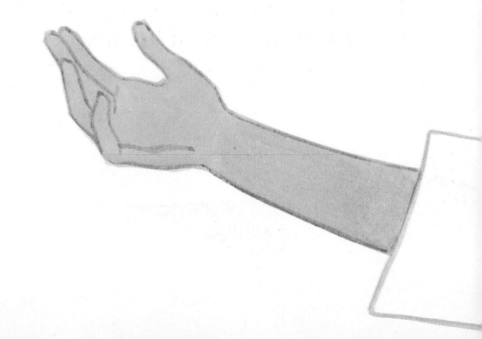

HAPPY ARE THOSE WHO MOURN;
GOD WILL COMFORT THEM!

When sorrow comes, and come it will,
For nothing stays the same—
Your playmate moves, old Rover dies,
Your Grandma's getting lame—

Remember that your Father knows
And loves you for your tears
Because they mean your loving heart
Shares human pain and fears.

And Father that He is, He'll make
A rainbow for His darling's sake!

HAPPY ARE THE MEEK;
THEY WILL HAVE WHAT
GOD HAS PROMISED!

Who are the meek? They're quite like you:
They're thoughtful-hearted children who
Don't whine and fuss or frown and pout
When Mother says, "You can't go out
Until you've put your toys away,"
Or Daddy says, "Some other day."

They try to understand and do
The kindly things God wants them to.
They will receive (as you can guess)
A share in God's own happiness!

HAPPY ARE THOSE WHOSE GREATEST
DESIRE IS TO DO WHAT GOD REQUIRES
GOD WILL SATISFY THEM FULLY!

It can be difficult to choose
The right above the wrong
(It's easier to hide from blame,
Or bully when you're strong).

But when you long with all your heart
To choose what's *truly* best
Because God asks this of His friends—
He'll make up for the rest.

He'll fill your life with peace and joy:
He'll fill your heart with song:
And you will have enough of love
To last a *heaven* long!

HAPPY ARE THOSE WHO ARE MERCIFUL TO OTHERS; GOD WILL BE MERCIFUL TO THEM!

There comes a time for everyone
(And, yes, for me and you)
When we will fail to do the good
God wants His children to.

We need the love and mercy
He will so gladly give
If only *we* are merciful
And willing to forgive.

And God makes certain, little one,
(As you will come to find)
Our *own* hearts brim with happiness
Whenever we are kind.

HAPPY ARE THE PURE IN HEART;
THEY WILL SEE GOD!

We are so wonderfully made,
With every sense just right
For finding all the gifts God gives
To fill us with delight:

Gifts to touch and taste and smell:
Gifts for ears and eyes.
The good God knew we needed them,
And He is *very* wise.

And when we use or share these gifts
With love and reverent care,
We'll sing a song of happiness
And see God *everywhere!*

HAPPY ARE THOSE WHO WORK
FOR PEACE AMONG MEN;
GOD WILL CALL THEM
HIS SONS!

God's work is peace. He wants all men
To live as brothers here
And help each other so that none
Need live in want or fear.

He needs us all to work with Him
(The grown-ups have *their* part)
So that the Kingdom of His love
Will come to *every* heart.

If we can be unselfish
And fair in work and play,
He'll call us sons and daughters
In quite a special way.

HAPPY ARE THOSE WHO ARE
PERSECUTED BECAUSE THEY DO
WHAT GOD REQUIRES;
THE KINGDOM
    OF HEAVEN BELONGS
        TO THEM!

God asks us to be truthful,
Kind, and pure, and just.
But sometimes it is very hard
To do the things we must—

Especially when playmates taunt,
Or tease, call names, or chide
(A window's broken, maybe,
And you won't run and hide).

But courage grows each time you choose
What God would want you to.
And can you guess the best of all?
Why, *Heaven* belongs to YOU!